VALUE BUILDERS

LOYAL & SELF-DISCIPLINED

Bible-based activities to strengthen Christian values

Copyright ©1995 David C. Cook Publishing Co. Printed in the United States of America.

All puzzles and Bible activities are based on the NIV.

Scripture taken from the Holy Bible, New International Version, Copyright ©1973, 1978, 1984, International Bible Society. Used by permission of Zondervan Bible Publishers.

ISBN: 0-7814-5105-1

Edited by Debbie Bible
Book Design by Jack Rogers
Cover Illustration by Corbin Hillam
Interior Illustrations by Dana Regan & Corbin Hillam

TABLE OF CONTENTS

INTRODUCTION FOR ADULT FRIENDS OF CHILDREN
(Parents, Teachers, and Other Friends of Children)

Values. What are they? How do we acquire them? Can we change them?

"Values" is a popular term, usually meaning *the standard that governs how one acts and conducts one's life.* Our personal standards, or values, are learned and adapted, possibly changed and relearned, over a lifetime of experiences and influences.

Children begin acquiring personal values at birth. As parents, teachers, and other adults who love children, we are concerned that they are learning worthwhile values, rather than being randomly influenced by everything around them. By God's design, we cannot control the process of acquiring values, but we can influence the process in a variety of ways. Our consistent modeling of biblical values is a vital influence, but children must also be encouraged to talk about specific values and be aware of these values in action in themselves and others.

These biblical values are God's values. He has established His standards to help us know how to live our lives and how we are to treat other people. Our goal is to have these biblical values be a part of each child's experience.

A value becomes one's own when a person chooses to act on that value consistently. Saying that we hold to the value of honesty, yet bending the truth or telling a lie when pressured, is a contradiction.

Providing opportunities for children to investigate a specific value, identifying with people in the Bible who have that value, and trying to put it into practice in real life situations will help strengthen the value in the lives of the children and reinforce its importance. The purpose of the Value Builders Series is to provide such opportunities.

This book in the Value Builders Series focuses on **being loyal** and **being self-disciplined**. Being loyal is *standing up for a friend or for what you believe even when it is hard.* Ruth is a biblical example of being loyal. She was a companion to Naomi and lived with Naomi's people rather than her own. Eventually, Ruth also accepted Naomi's God as her own. Another example is Jonathan, who remained loyal to his friend, David. Jonathan showed his loyalty by warning David when it became too dangerous for David to stay near King Saul.

Being self-disciplined is *making yourself do what you know you should do, even when you don't feel like doing it.* Daniel did what he knew he should do when he and the other men were prisoners of King Nebuchadnezzar. Daniel asked to defy

the King's orders and be served food that wouldn't be dishonorable to God. Jesus is another example of being self-disciplined. In silence, He endured the sarcasm and mockery from the soldiers as he stood before the crowd that was calling for his death.

The Value Builders Series provides Bible story activities, craft activities, and life application activities that focus on specific biblical values. These books can be used by children working alone, or the pages can be reproduced and used in a classroom setting.

In a classroom setting, this book could be used to supplement curriculum that you are using, or it can be used as a curriculum itself in a 30-55 minute period. Each page is coded at the bottom to suggest where it might fit in a teaching session. The codes are as follows:

 = Definition page

 = Bible Story page

= Craft page

= Life Application page

Some suggestions for using the materials in this book in a 30-55 minute period are:

5-10 minutes:	Introduce the value and discuss the definition. Use pages entitled, "What Is Being Loyal?" or "What Is Being Self-Disciplined?"
10-15 minutes:	Present one of the Bible stories, using appropriate pages. Encourage the children to describe what it might have been like to be in that situation and what other things could have happened.
10-20 minutes:	Choose life application activity pages or craft activities that are appropriate to the children in your class. Design some group applications for the pages you have chosen.
5-10 minutes:	To conclude, use the page entitled, "The Value of Being Loyal" or "The Value of Being Self-Disciplined" and encourage the children to make a commitment to focus on this value for the next few days or weeks. Pray for God's help to guide the children as they learn to live by His standards.

WHAT IS BEING LOYAL?

BEING LOYAL IS...standing up for a friend or for what you believe even when it is hard to do so.

I think being loyal can also mean _____

_____

✎ **Put a check mark on the line if you think the statement is telling about being loyal.**

Being loyal is . . .

YES   NO

____ ____ walking away from your friends when they call you to help.

____ ____ speaking up for friends when they are being teased.

____ ____ saying you don't go to church when you really do go.

____ ____ telling someone that you believe Jesus is the Son of God.

Being loyal is important to me.
When I stand up for a friend and stay true to what I believe even when it is hard, then being loyal becomes one of my values.

Name _____

Date _____

God's values are the STANDARD to help me know how to live my life and treat other people

THE BIBLE TELLS ABOUT BEING LOYAL

Ruth Is Loyal and Stays with Naomi

Ruth 1:1-22

"FAMINE" MEANS NOT ENOUGH FOOD FOR THE PEOPLE AND ANIMALS.

In the days when the judges ruled, there was a famine in the land, and a man [Elimelech] from Bethlehem in Judah, together with his wife [Naomi] and two sons, went to live for a while in the country of Moab. . . .

Now Elimelech, Naomi's husband, died, and she was left with her two sons [Mahlon and Kilion]. They married Moabite women, one named Orpah and the other Ruth. After they had lived there about ten years, both Mahlon and Kilion also died, and Naomi was left without her two sons and her husband.

When she heard in Moab that the LORD had come to the aid of his people by providing food for them, Naomi and her daughters-in-law prepared to return home from there. With her two daughters-in-law she left the place where she had been living and set out on the road that would take them back to the land of Judah.

Then Naomi said to her two daughters-in-law, "Go back, each of you, to your mother's home. May the LORD show kindness to you, as you have shown to your dead and to me. . . ."

(Read the rest of this story on page 7)

✎ **Use these words to finish the sentences about Ruth. Some words may be used twice.**

stay   go   God
people   loyal

1. Ruth was __ __ __ __ __ to Naomi.

2. Ruth wanted to __ __ where Naomi was going to __ __ and to

__ __ __ __ where Naomi would __ __ __ __ .

3. Ruth said that Naomi's __ __ __ __ __ __ would be

her __ __ __ __ __ __ .

4. Ruth decided to serve and believe in Naomi's __ __ __ .

6

Ruth Is Loyal and Stays with Naomi

(Ruth 1:1-22 continued from page 6)

Then she kissed them and they wept aloud and said to her, "We will go back with you to your people."

"WEPT" MEANS THEY CRIED.

But Naomi said, "Return home, my daughters. Why would you come with me? Am I going to have any more sons, who could become your husbands? Return home, my daughters . . ."

At this they wept again. Then Orpah kissed her mother-in-law good-by, but Ruth clung to her.

"Look," said Naomi, "your sister-in-law is going back to her people and her gods. Go back with her."

But Ruth replied, "Don't urge me to leave you or to turn back from you. Where you go I will go, and where you stay I will stay. Your people will be my people and your God my God. . . ." When Naomi realized that Ruth was determined to go with her, she stopped urging her.

"STIRRED" MEANS EXCITED.

So the two women went on until they came to Bethlehem. When they arrived in Bethlehem, the whole town was stirred because of them, and the women exclaimed, "Can this be Naomi?" . . .

So Naomi returned from Moab accompanied by Ruth . . . arriving in Bethlehem as the barley harvest was beginning.

✎ **Write the number from the map to show where each thing happened. Some numbers may be used more than once.**

_____ There was not enough food here and so Elimelech, Naomi, and their sons had to leave.

_____ Naomi lived here with her sons and their wives, Ruth and Orpah.

_____ Ruth and Naomi went back to Naomi's homeland.

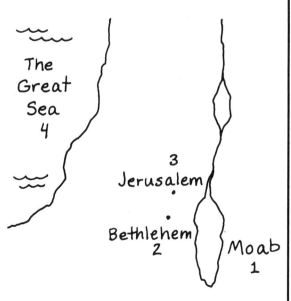

Ruth Is Loyal and Stays with Naomi

✏ **Read about Ruth and Naomi in your Bible in Ruth 1:1-22 or on pages 6 and 7. Use the code to find the words to finish the story.**

CODE:
❂ =Bethlehem   ✳ =Elimelech   ● =food   ○ =loyal

■ =Moab   ❑ =Naomi   ▲ =Orpah   ◆ =Ruth   ❖ =sons

In _____ , in the land of Judah, there was not enough
       ❂

_____ for _____ , _____ ,
   ●   ✳   ❑

and their two _____ . The family decided to go to _____
       ❖   ■

to live. Later, in _____ , _____ died. The
          ■   ✳

two _____ grew up and married young women named _____
     ❖   ◆

and _____ . Some years later, both of the _____ died
    ▲   ❖

and _____ , _____ and _____ were left alone.
    ❑   ◆   ▲

_____ decided to go back to her home in _____
   ❑   ❂

where there was now plenty of _____ . _____ wanted to be
                      ●   ◆

with _____ . _____ was _____ to _____ and
    ❑   ◆   ○   ❑

went with _____ on the long trip back to _____ .
     ❑   ❂

A PRAYER ABOUT BEING LOYAL TO GOD

✎ **Use these words to fill in the Bible verse from 1 Chronicles 29:18. Some words may be used more than once.**

A and Abraham	D desire	F fathers forever	G God	H hearts	I in Isaac Israel
K keep	L Lord loyal	O of our	P people	T the their this to	Y you your

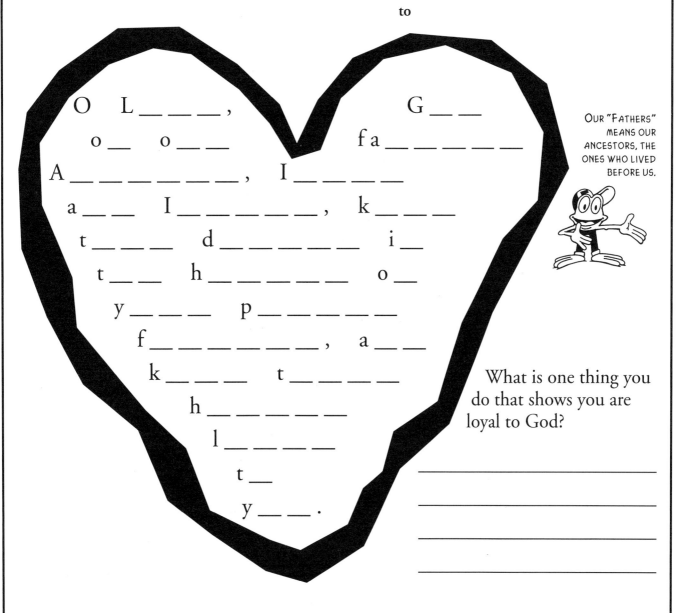

O L _ _ _ ,   G _ _

o _   o _ _   f a _ _ _ _ _ _

A _ _ _ _ _ _ _ ,   I _ _ _ _ _

a _ _   I _ _ _ _ _ _ ,   k _ _ _

t _ _ _ _   d _ _ _ _ _ _   i _

t _ _   h _ _ _ _ _ _   o _

y _ _ _   p _ _ _ _ _

f _ _ _ _ _ _ _ ,   a _ _

k _ _ _ _   t _ _ _ _ _

h _ _ _ _ _ _

l _ _ _ _ _

t _

y _ _ .

OUR "FATHERS" MEANS OUR ANCESTORS, THE ONES WHO LIVED BEFORE US.

What is one thing you do that shows you are loyal to God?

_____
_____
_____
_____

WHEN IT IS HARD TO BE LOYAL

Sometimes it is hard to be loyal. Read about Carol and Brady and then write what you think they will say.

Carol wants to be loyal to her church and to what she believes about Jesus. What do you think Carol will say?

_____

_____

_____

LOOK! THAT GUY REALLY DOES HAVE A LOT OF HAIR!

BUT HIS FRIEND IS LOYAL TO HIM.

Brady wants to be loyal to his friend, Barry, but he also wants to be friends with those who don't like Barry. What do you think Brady will say?

_____

_____

_____

STANDING UP FOR A FRIEND

Jerry's friend, Myrone, was always teased about his size when Jerry and Myrone walked by the older kids. If Jerry continues to walk with Myrone, he might eventually get teased about something, too. Should he keep walking with Myrone or go another way? ✎ **If Jerry wants to be a loyal friend to Myrone, which path will Jerry choose? Draw a line to show your choice.**

LOYAL FRIENDS
WORK TOGETHER

The words to the Bible verse, Romans 12:5 are scattered on this page. Draw a line to connect the words—and circle each word as you come to it. But DO NOT touch or cross another line to get to the next word. Look before you draw a line; you may have to go the long way around.

SO
1

MANY
7

CHRIST
3

"BELONG TO EACH OTHER" MEANS TO HELP EACH OTHER WHEN YOU CAN.

IN
2

ARE
6

ONE
9

WHO
5

FORM
8

THE
17

BODY,
10

WE
4

AND
11

ALL
16

MEMBER
13

BELONGS
14

OTHERS
18

EACH
12

TO
15

The "body of Christ" is the church. What are some ways you can be loyal to someone at church? _____

_____

SHOW YOU ARE LOYAL WITH A GIFT

Make two Cover-ups and give one to a friend as a sign that you will be loyal.

For each Cover-up, you will need:
- ☐ 1 bath towel
- ☐ 1 hand or fingertip towel
- ☐ Needle and thread or a sewing machine
- ☐ OPTIONAL: Pins

✂ **To make a Cover-up:**

1. Fold the small towel in half and stitch along one side. (See illustration.)

2. Turn this towel so the seam is on the inside. This part will be a hood to cover the top of your head.

3. Fold the large towel in half to find the middle point. Put a pin at that spot on one edge.

4. Mark the middle point of the unsewn side of the small towel in the same way.

5. Put the two towels together at the middle points with the outsides facing. (The outsides are the sides that will be on the outside when you wear the Cover-up.) Stitch together along the length of the small towel.

6. Put the hood of your Cover-up on your head and the rest of it around your shoulders.

7. Give your gift to a friend and show how it can be used to keep you warm after you have been swimming together.

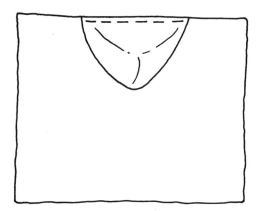

THE BIBLE TELLS ABOUT BEING LOYAL

The King's Son, Jonathan, Is Loyal

1 Samuel 18:3-9, 29; 20:1-42

Jonathan made a covenant with David because he loved him as himself. . . .

Whatever [King] Saul sent him to do, David did it so successfully that Saul gave him a high rank in the army. This pleased all the people, and Saul's officers as well. . . . And from that time on Saul kept a jealous eye on David. . . .

Saul became still more afraid of him, and he remained his enemy the rest of his days.

Then David fled from Naioth at Ramah and went to Jonathan and asked, "What have I done? What is my crime? How have I wronged your father [King Saul], that he is trying to take my life?" . . .

Jonathan said to David, "Whatever you want me to do, I'll do for you."

So David said, "Look, tomorrow . . . I am supposed to dine with the king; but let me go and hide in the field until the evening of the day after tomorrow. If your father misses me at all, tell him, 'David earnestly asked my permission to hurry to Bethlehem, his hometown . . .' If he says, 'Very well,' then [I am] safe. But if he loses his temper, you can be sure that he is determined to harm me. . . ."

Then Jonathan said to David: ". . . The day after tomorrow, toward evening, go to the place where you hid when this trouble began, and wait by the stone Ezel. I will shoot three arrows to the side of it, as though I were shooting at a target. . . . But if I say to the boy, 'Look, the arrows are beyond you,' then you must go . . ."

(Read the rest of this story on page 15)

✎ **Write the missing vowels.**

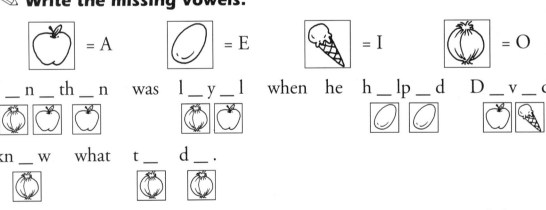

J _ n _ th _ n   was   l _ y _ l   when he   h _ lp _ d   D _ v _ d

kn _ w   what   t _ d _ .

J _ n _ th _ n   gave   a   m _ ss _ g _   to   D _ v _ d by

sh _ _ t _ ng   the   _ rr _ ws beyond   the   r _ ck.

THE BIBLE TELLS ABOUT BEING LOYAL

The King's Son, Jonathan, Is Loyal

(1 Samuel 18:3-9, 29; 20:1-42 continued from page 14)

So David hid in the field, and when . . . the king sat down to eat . . . David's place was empty. Saul said nothing that day . . . But the next day . . . David's place was empty again. Then Saul said to his son Jonathan, "Why hasn't [David] come to the meal, either yesterday or today?"

Jonathan answered, "David earnestly asked me for permission to go to Bethlehem. . . . That is why he has not come to the king's table."

Saul's anger flared up at Jonathan and he said to him, ". . . Now send and bring him to me, for he must die!"

"Why should he be put to death? What has he done?" Jonathan asked his father. But Saul hurled his spear at him to kill him. Then Jonathan knew that his father intended to kill David.

Jonathan got up from the table in fierce anger; on that second day of the month he did not eat, because he was grieved . . .

In the morning Jonathan went out to the field for his meeting with David. He had a small boy with him, and he said to the boy, "Run and find the arrows I shoot." As the boy ran . . . Jonathan called out after him, "Isn't the arrow beyond you?" Then he shouted, "Hurry! Go quickly! Don't stop!" . . .

After the boy had gone, David got up from the south side and bowed down before Jonathan three times, with his face to the ground. Then they kissed each other and wept together—but David wept the most.

Jonathan said to David, "Go in peace, for we have sworn friendship with each other in the name of the LORD . . ." Then David left. . . .

✎ **In each group circle the word that appears in the Bible story. Then find the word in each group that doesn't go with the other words and mark through it.**

covenant
promise
angry
agree

eat together
sleep
dine
meal

faithful
loyal
sworn friendship
be mean to

laughing
wept
crying
sad

THE BIBLE TELLS
ABOUT BEING LOYAL

The King's Son, Jonathan, Is Loyal

✎ **Read about David and Jonathan in your Bible in 1 Samuel 18:3-9, 29; 20:1-42 or on pages 14 and 15. Draw a line to the picture that answers each question.**

1. Who asked why David didn't come to eat at the King's table?

David

2. Who hid in the field?

3. Who was very jealous of David and wanted to kill him?

4. Who said, "Whatever you want me to do, I'll do for you?"

Jonathan

5. Who shot three arrows?

6. Who ran to pick up the arrows?

King Saul

7. Who cried the most because he had to leave his loyal friend?

A "COVENANT" IS AGREEING TO KEEP A PROMISE.

DAVID AND JONATHAN AGREED TO STAY LOYAL TO EACH OTHER.

Boy

PUPPETS FOR A
PLAY ABOUT BEING LOYAL

Cut out the puppets, sign, and props to use with the puppet play on pages 19 and 20.

You need:
- ☐ 4 paper strips 1/2" x 11" for legs
- ☐ 4 paper strips 1/2" x 8-1/2" for arms
- ☐ Glue
- ☐ 2-4" length of string

✂ **To make the arms and legs for the puppets:**

1. Put the ends of two paper strips of the same length at right angles, as shown, and glue these ends together.
2. Fold the strips back and forth over each other to make a "spring" or flexible length.
3. Make two "springs" for arms and two for legs for each puppet.
4. Glue one end of the "springs" in place on the puppet and glue a hand or foot at the other end.

✂ **To make a bow:**

1. Cut out the bow or photocopy the pattern.
2. Put a knot in one end of the string and slip it into the notch at one end of the bow.
3. Put the other end of the string in the notched end at the other end of the bow, pulling it gently. Knot that end of the string or tape it in place so the bow keeps its shape.

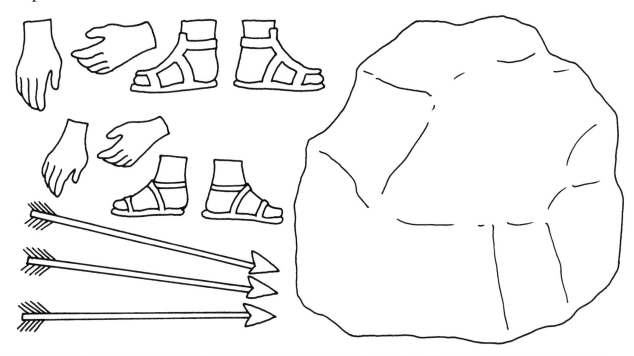

PUPPETS FOR A PLAY
ABOUT BEING LOYAL

DAVID

JONATHAN

MIKE

TWO DAYS LATER

FOLD

FOLD

DAVID AND HIS LOYAL FRIEND

A Puppet Play Based on 1 Samuel 20:1-42

In this true story are: David, Jonathan, and a young boy we'll call Mike

PREPARATION: 1. Follow the directions for making the puppets and props on pages 17 and 18.
2. You may want to add background pieces such as the king's palace and some trees and small shrubs.

SETTING: This takes place in the fields outside the city of Jerusalem.

[DAVID enters stage right and talks to audience.]

DAVID: I have a problem! Maybe you can give me some advice. You see, it's like this. I've been serving King Saul, first in his palace and now in his army. The good part is, that's how I met the king's son, Jonathan. We really hit it off and got to be such good friends But, now, Jonathan's dad, King Saul, wants me out of here. He doesn't like the way I've been doing such a good job as a soldier—even though he was the one who made me a leader in the army!

So, here's the problem. *(DAVID walks to center stage and leans out and whispers.)* I'm supposed to eat with the king at a celebration feast. Even though the king thinks I'm a threat to his position and wants to get rid of me, do I still honor him and go to dinner?

[JONATHAN enters left and looks around. DAVID glances toward the left and turns back to the audience.]

DAVID: Oh, there's Jonathan. I'll go ask him what he thinks. I KNOW I can count on him. *(Calls loudly.)* Hey, Jonathan! *(JONATHAN and DAVID move toward each other and stop to talk.)* Did you know that Your father is so angry at me that he is trying to take my life?

JONATHAN: Oh, I don't think so, David. My father wouldn't keep that from me.

DAVID: Sure he would. He knows we are friends. He wouldn't want you to know about it. The point is—what do I do now?

JONATHAN: I'm still not sure, but if I can help you, let me know.

DAVID: Thanks! Here's an idea. Tomorrow I am supposed to have dinner with the king. But I'm afraid to go. Instead, since you will be there, notice if your father misses me. If he asks you about me, tell him that you gave me permission to go somewhere. If he says, 'Very well,' then I'll know I'm safe. But if he loses his temper, even you will know that he is determined to harm me.

DAVID AND HIS LOYAL FRIEND

JONATHAN: OK, let's do it. I'll signal you like this. In the evening, the day after tomorrow, you go to the field where you hid before and wait by the big stone. I will shoot three arrows to the side of the stone, as though I were shooting at a target. If you hear me say to the boy who goes after my arrows, "Look, the arrows are beyond you," then you will know you are right about the danger from my father.

DAVID: You are a loyal friend, Jonathan. I'll see you in two days. *(JONATHAN exits left and DAVID exits right.)*

[Put up sign TWO DAYS later and a large stone is placed on the right side. DAVID is hiding behind the stone. JONATHAN enters left carrying a bow, followed by MIKE holding arrows.]

JONATHAN: This looks like a good place for target practice, Mike. I can use that rock as a target. After I shoot some, you run and find them for me. *(JONATHAN puts an arrow in the bow and shoots it beyond the rock. Then he shoots two more the same way. MIKE starts running toward where the arrows landed and JONATHAN calls.)* Isn't the arrow beyond you? *(He yells louder.)* Hurry! Go quickly! Don't stop!

(MIKE starts running faster, thinking JONATHAN was talking to him. MIKE picks up the arrows and runs back to JONATHAN.) Terrific! Thanks, Mike. Please take the bow and arrows back to the palace. *(MIKE runs off stage left, carrying the bow and arrows.)*

[DAVID moves from behind the rock and walks slowly left, bowing before JONATHAN three times, as if JONATHAN were the king.]

DAVID: Oh, Jonathan, you are the king's Son and you should be king some day. But you have been loyal and warned me about the danger. Obviously, your father was angry that I didn't come to the feast.

JONATHAN: Yes, you were right, David. At first he didn't say anything, but I could tell he noticed you were gone. At the second feast, he asked me about you. When I told him you were away, he got angry. He wanted me to find you and bring you to him. Why, he even threw his spear at me! I got out of there fast. I'm so ashamed that my father would treat you this way after all you have done for him and our country. This is such a sad day, but you really must leave here. It isn't safe. *(JONATHAN and DAVID start to cry. They hug each other.)* Go in peace. We will still be friends and stay loyal to each other even when we are far apart.

[DAVID walks slowly with his head down to exit on stage right, while JONATHAN slowly exits stage left.]

MAKE A LOYAL DOCUMENT

Make your own pens and write a document to show that you will be loyal.

You need:
- ☐ A large feather from a goose or turkey, or a dried reed or bamboo stem about 1/4" diameter
- ☐ Knife
- ☐ Parchment paper or other special paper, 8-1/2" x 11"
- ☐ Ink or paint

LOOK! THE KIDS ARE COMING TO OUR POND TO GET REEDS.

LET'S HELP THEM.

✂ To make a pen point:

1. Have an adult help you cut the end of your feather or reed. Make a scoop-like cut on the underside.
2. Cut each side of the end to make a point.
3. Cut a short slit in the middle of the tip.
4. OPTIONAL: If you have extra feathers, make different angles on each one and experiment to see which kind works the best.

Step I

Step 2

Step 3

✂ To make a Loyal Document:

1. Decide what words to write on your document. Choose something that will say WHO you will be loyal to, and have a place to sign your name.

FOR EXAMPLE:

> I, _____ ,
> (write your name here)
> will keep myself
> loyal
> to God and the Bible.
> _____
> (write the date here.)

2. Dip your pen point into the ink or paint and write the words on your special paper.
3. Keep your Loyal Document in a safe place to remind you of your promise to stay loyal.

JESUS WILL HELP YOU BE LOYAL

✏️ **Each word under a picture is hidden in the word hunt. Find and circle each one.**

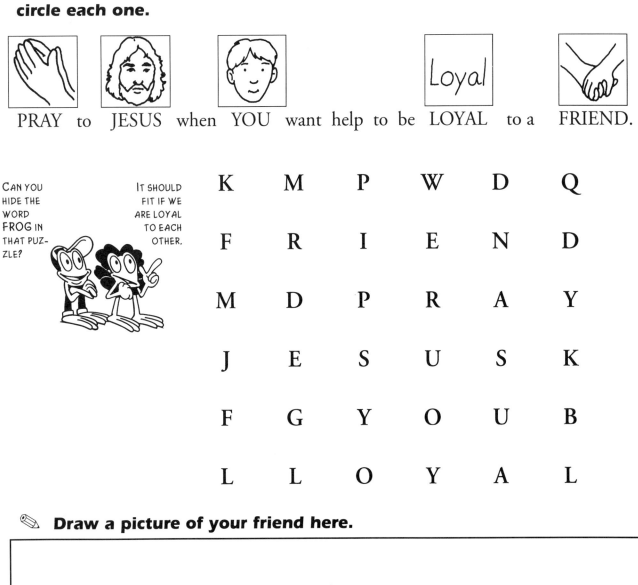

PRAY to JESUS when YOU want help to be LOYAL to a FRIEND.

CAN YOU HIDE THE WORD FROG IN THAT PUZZLE?

IT SHOULD FIT IF WE ARE LOYAL TO EACH OTHER.

K	M	P	W	D	Q
F	R	I	E	N	D
M	D	P	R	A	Y
J	E	S	U	S	K
F	G	Y	O	U	B
L	L	O	Y	A	L

✏️ **Draw a picture of your friend here.**

THE VALUE OF BEING LOYAL

God's values are the STANDARD to help me know how to live my life and treat other people

HOW CAN YOU KNOW WHAT YOUR VALUES ARE?

Look at the things you DO, SAY, and THINK. If you spend time doing something, then you know it is one of your values.

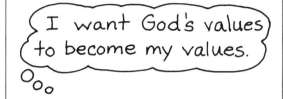

I want God's values to become my values.

✎ Draw a picture of yourself here.
Are you thinking what is in the thought balloon?

My name is _____

Being loyal _____ important to me.
                 is   is not

I _____ spend time standing up for my friends and for what I believe even
     do   do not

when it is hard.

Standing up for a friend or for what you believe even when it is hard is being loyal.

I can show that being loyal is becoming my value when I _____

_____ and _____

✎ **Use fabric crayons or paints to decorate a visor with the slogan, "You can count on me!"**

BEING SELF-DISCIPLINED IS . . . making yourself do what you know you should do even when you don't feel like it.

I think being self-disciplined can also mean _____

_____

✎ **Hold this page up to the mirror to see what you need to do next.**

What are two things you should do even when you don't feel like it? Write those words on the lines below.

_____

_____

Being self-disciplined is important to me.
When I spend time doing what I know I should do, even when I don't feel like doing it, then being self-disciplined becomes one of my values.

Name _____

Date _____

God's values are the STANDARD to help me know how to live my life and treat other people

Daniel Honors God about the King's Food

Daniel and other young men were taken as prisoners and forced to live in Babylon and serve King Nebuchadnezzar.

Daniel 1:1-20

. . . Nebuchadnezzar king of Babylon came to Jerusalem and besieged it. . . .

Then the king ordered Ashpenaz, chief of his court officials, to bring in some of the Israelites . . . young men without any physical defect, handsome, showing aptitude for every kind of learning, well informed, quick to understand, and qualified to serve in the king's palace. He was to teach them the language and literature of the Babylonians. The king assigned them a daily amount of food . . . from the king's table. They were to be trained for three years, and after that they were to enter the king's service.

Among these were some from Judah: Daniel . . . Shadrach . . . Meshach and . . . Abednego.

"BESIEGED" MEANS THE CITY WAS SURROUNDED AND UNDER ATTACK BY SOLDIERS.

"DEFILED" MEANS TO MAKE UNCLEAN. IT'S LIKE BEING DIRTY INSIDE.

But Daniel resolved not to defile himself with the royal food . . . and he asked the chief official for permission not to defile himself this way. Now God had caused the official to show favor and sympathy to Daniel, but the official told Daniel, "I am afraid of my lord the king, who has assigned your food and drink. Why should he see you looking worse than the other young men your age? The king would then have my head because of you."

(Read the rest of this story on page 26)

✎ **Look in the Bible story and do these things.**

1. Draw a circle around the names of the men from Judah.

2. Make a box around the words that tell what Daniel decided (resolved) to do regarding the king's food.

3. Make a line under the name of the king.

Daniel Honors God about the King's Food

(Daniel 1:1-20 continued from page 25)

Daniel then said to the guard whom the chief official had appointed over [them], "Please test [us] for ten days: Give us nothing but vegetables to eat and water to drink. Then compare our appearance with that of the young men who eat the royal food, and treat [us] in accordance with what you see." So he agreed to this and tested them for ten days.

THE KING'S MEAT WAS NOT PREPARED THE WAY GOD'S LAW SAID IT SHOULD BE.

At the end of the ten days they looked healthier and better nourished than any of the young men who ate the royal food. So the guard took away their choice food . . . and gave them vegetables instead.

To these four young men God gave knowledge and understanding of all kinds of literature and learning. And Daniel could understand visions and dreams of all kinds.

AND SOME OF IT HAD BEEN OFFERED TO IDOLS. NO WONDER DANIEL SAID IT WOULD BE WRONG TO EAT IT!

At the end of the time set by the king to bring them in, the chief official presented them to Nebuchadnezzar. The king talked with them, and he found none equal to Daniel, [Shadrach, Meshach, and Abednego]; so they entered the king's service. In every matter of wisdom and understanding about which the king questioned them, he found them ten times better than all . . . in his whole kingdom.

✎ **Draw a line from each name to the sentences that tell about that person.**

Daniel

Guard

Nebuchadnezzar

Ashpenaz

Ashpenaz appointed this person to oversee the men.

He was the king.

He was the chief official.

He was self-disciplined and wouldn't eat the food God's law said not to eat.

He was afraid of the king.

He agreed to test the men for ten days.

Daniel Honors God about the King's Food

✎ **Read about Daniel in your Bible in Daniel 1:1-20 or on pages 25 and 26. Follow the directions below.**

① You're right, we won't go against God's law and eat the royal food. I'll go talk to the Chief Official, Ashpenaz.

Draw a circle around Daniel.

② But if you get weak and sick, I'll get in trouble with the King. I can't do it.

Write what Daniel said to Ashpenaz.

③ Please give us only _____ and _____ for the next ten days.

Write the two missing words here:

④ TEN DAYS LATER

Draw a picture or write about what happened next.

⑤ THREE YEARS LATER

Write what the king said about Daniel and his friends.

✎ **Some of the words to the Bible verse, 1 Timothy 4:7, 8, are hidden in this box of letters. Follow the letters this way.** **START** **Write the words below.**

START

T	L	F	C	A	O	M	I	N	L	T
R	E	G	I	L	S	E	L	E	L	H
A	S	O	S	T	G	V	D	S	A	I
I	R	D	Y	R	N	A	O	S	E	N
N	U	L	H	A	I	L	G	V	U	G
Y	O	Y	P	I	N	U	E	A	L	S

T __ __ __ __   __ __ __ __ __ __ __ __ __ __   to be

__ __ __ __ __ __ . For __ __ __ __ __ __ __ __ __

__ __ __ __ __ __ __ __ __   is of __ __ __ __ __

__ __ __ __ __ __ __ , but __ __ __ __ __ __ __ __ __

has __ __ __ __ __ __   for __ __ __ __   __ __ __ __ __ __ __ __ .

✎ **Draw lines to match the meanings to these words in the Bible verse.**

PHYSICAL TRAINING	SOME VALUE	TRAIN	GODLINESS
doing things God's way	practice, keep on doing it	important, but not the most important thing	exercise your body, arms, and legs

What are some things you can do to train yourself to do what God wants you to do?

_____

SELF-DISCIPLINED IS ABOUT YOURSELF

✎ **When you see a ☐ draw a picture of yourself or write your name. Follow the trail from each letter and write that letter in the box at the end of the trail to read the message.**

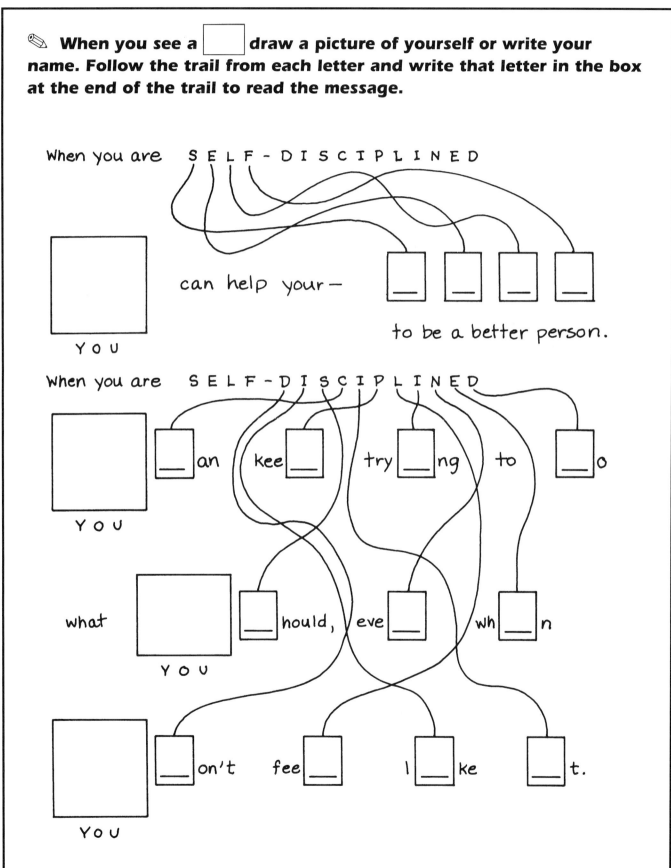

When you are S E L F - D I S C I P L I N E D

☐
YOU

can help your— ☐ ☐ ☐ ☐

to be a better person.

When you are S E L F - D I S C I P L I N E D

☐
YOU

___an kee___ try___ng to ___o

what ☐
YOU

___hould, eve___ wh___n

☐
YOU

___on't fee___ l___ke ___t.

STICKS AND DIPS ARE GOOD TO EAT

Make some sticks and dips to enjoy with your lunch. When you eat the things you know you should, you are practicing being self-disciplined in your diet.

I SEE SOME FROG'S LEGS IN THE LUNCH!

THEY ARE ATTACHED TO ME! THIS IS GOOD DIP!

You need:
- ☐ 1/2 cup plain yogurt
- ☐ 1/2 cup light sour cream
- ☐ 1/2 cup applesauce
- ☐ 3 carrots, cut into 3" "sticks"
- ☐ 1 apple, cut into thin "sticks"
- ☐ 1 spoon
- ☐ OPTIONAL: Other vegetables and fruits of your choice

- ☐ 1 tsp. dried onion soup OR 1 tsp. fresh dill
- ☐ 3 celery stalks, cut into 3" "sticks"
- ☐ 2 cheese slices, cut into "sticks"
- ☐ 3 small dishes or the Stick Dip Holder

✄ To make Sticks and Dips:
1. Mix the dill or onion soup mix into the sour cream.
2. Put the yogurt, sour cream mixture, and applesauce into three different small bowls.

✄ To enjoy Sticks and Dips:
Dip a stick into a dip of sauce and stick it in your mouth! Share your Sticks and Dips with your friends.

Make a Stick Dip Holder

You need:
- ☐ 1 clean plastic egg carton
- ☐ Scissors
- ☐ 1-3 long chenille wire(s)

✄ To make a Stick Dip Holder:
1. To make three holders, cut the egg carton into three separate pieces, with four egg cups in each piece.
2. To make a handle for your holder, push one end of the chenille wire into the space where the four egg cups meet and through to the other side of the container.
3. Push the other end of the wire through the carton close to the same place where the first end was inserted and twist around the first wire end. Form a carrying handle.
4. Put the dips into the Stick Dip Holder and serve it with your sticks of vegetables, fruit and cheese.

LEARNING TO BE SELF-DISCIPLINED

Being self-disciplined takes a lot of practice. Here are some ways to help you learn about it. ✎ **Follow the directions in each section.**

GRANDMA GREEN HAS A LOT OF SELF-DISCIPLINE.

IS THAT BEING FROG-DISCIPLINED?

A. Think about someone you know who shows self-discipline.

✎ **Write that person's name here.** _____

Ask that person about how TO WANT to make yourself do the things you should, when you don't feel like it.

✎ **Write two things that person said you might do:**

_____

_____

B. Read these Bible verses that tell about how important it is to be self-disciplined.

✎ **Put a check on the line after you read each verse.**

_____ Ephesians 4:29

_____ Proverbs 23:4

_____ Galatians 5:22,23

_____ 2 Corinthians 8:21

C. Ask God to help you. God knows the things that are hard for you to do and He wants to help you be self-disciplined.

✎ **Write your prayer here.**

_____

_____

BE SELF-DISCIPLINED EVERY DAY

What do you think is in this picture? ✎ **Follow the color code to find out.**

1–Brown   2–Orange   3–Red   4–Blue   5–Green   6–Black

How is this child showing self-discipline?

IS IT EASY OR HARD FOR YOU?

Sometimes doing the things we should do is easy. But sometimes it takes self-discipline to do what we know we should do. ✎ **Read this list and put a check to show what is easy or hard for you to do.**

	EASY FOR ME	HARD FOR ME I'll practice self-discipline.
Helping with the dishes without being asked.		
Being a friend to someone the other kids laugh at.		
Not copying in a test when someone's answers are in plain sight.		
Putting things away when I stop working with them.		
Not going along with others who are doing something wrong.		
Stop talking to my friend when the teacher says, "Quiet".		
Telling the truth when a lie would be easier.		
Finishing my homework before I play.		

Look at the checks you made in the HARD FOR ME column. What can you do when you need self-discipline?

_____

✎ **Circle one area that you will practice being self-disciplined in.**

TV   homework   food   radio

computer games   exercise   video   music

reading   chores   temper   other: _____

✎ **Unscramble the missing words in the Bible verse 2 Timothy 1:7. Use the Word Box if you need help. Some words may be used more than once. Write the letters in the boxes on the lines at the bottom of the page to finish the sentence.**

For ☐ __ __   __ __☐ not give us a __ __ __ __ __ __☐
    (oGd)   (ddi)   (irtisp)

☐__ __ __ __ __ __ __ __☐ , but a __ __ __ __ __ __
(fo)   (diimtyti)   (irtisp)

☐__ __ ☐☐ __ __ , of love __ ☐ __ of
(fo)   (weorp)   (dna)

☐☐☐☐ - ☐☐☐☐☐☐☐☐☐☐☐ .
        (fels lpiesdiicn)

┌───┐
│ WORD   did   God   and   of   │
│ BOX   power   self-discipline spirit timidity │
└───┘

Ask __ o __   __ __

help __ __ u gr __ __ i __

__ __ __ __ - __ __ __ __ __ __ __ __ __ __ .

What are some tasks that are hard for you to be self-disciplined in?

_____

RATING WHAT YOU SEE AND READ

Everything you see and read becomes a part of who you are and what you think and do every day. The Bible teaches us in Philippians 4:8* to think about the things that are helpful to us. Here is a way to help you grow in self-discipline regarding what you watch and read.

✏ **Use a photocopier to make this chart bigger. Cut it out and paste it on a large piece of construction paper. Decorate it to be a poster and put it up in your room. When you read or watch something, write it on the chart.**

Write titles here:	Write YES or NO to answer each question.				
TV SHOWS MOVIES VIDEOS COMIC BOOKS BOOKS	Is it TRUE or HONEST about how things should be?	Is it PURE? (no bad language or wrong actions)	Can it be ADMIRED?	Is it EXCELLENT?	Can I say GOOD THINGS about it?

* Philippians 4:8
"Whatever is true, whatever is noble, whatever is right, whatever is pure, whatever is lovely, whatever is admirable—if anything is excellent or praiseworthy—think about such things."

THE BIBLE TELLS ABOUT BEING SELF-DISCIPLINED

Jesus Is Quiet When People Make Fun of Him

Matthew 27:1-31; John 19:16-42

Early in the morning, all the chief priests and the elders of the people came to the decision to put Jesus to death. They bound him, led him away and handed him over to Pilate, the governor. . . .

The governor asked him, "Are you the king of the Jews?"

"Yes, it is as you say," Jesus replied.

When he was accused by the chief priests and the elders, he gave no answer. Then Pilate asked him, "Don't you hear the testimony they are bringing against you?" But Jesus made no reply, not even to a single charge—to the great amazement of the governor. . . .

Then the governor's soldiers took Jesus into the Praetorium and gathered the whole company of soldiers around him. They stripped him and put a scarlet robe on him, and then twisted together a crown of thorns and set it on his head. They put a staff in his right hand and knelt in front of him and mocked him. "Hail, king of the Jews!" they said. They spit on him, and took the staff and struck him on the head again and again. After they had mocked him, they took off the robe and put his own clothes on him. Then they led him away to crucify him. . . .

"CRUCIFY" MEANS TO KILL BY HANGING ON A CROSS.

(Read the rest of this story on page 37)

(Read the rest of this story on page 37)

✎ **Draw a line to match the meanings with the words from the Bible story.**

1. bound   laughed at and made
                        fun of

2. mocked   not saying anything as
                        an answer

3. accused   tied up

4. made no reply   said he did things against
                        the law

THE BIBLE TELLS ABOUT BEING SELF-DISCIPLINED

Jesus Is Quiet When People Make Fun of Him

(Matthew 27:1-31; John 19:16-42 continued from page 36)

So the soldiers took charge of Jesus. Carrying his own cross, he went out to the place of the Skull (which in Aramaic is called Golgotha). Here they crucified him, and with him two others—one on each side and Jesus in the middle.

Pilate had a notice prepared and fastened to the cross. It read: JESUS OF NAZARETH, THE KING OF THE JEWS. . . .

Later, Joseph of Arimathea asked Pilate for the body of Jesus. Now Joseph was a disciple of Jesus, but secretly because he feared the Jews. With Pilate's permission, he came and took the body away. . . . At the place where Jesus was crucified, there was a garden, and in the garden a new tomb, in which no one had ever been laid. Because it was the Jewish day of Preparation and since the tomb was nearby, they laid Jesus there.

WHAT ABOUT THE REST OF THE STORY?

JESUS DIDN'T STAY DEAD. HE CAME BACK TO LIFE THREE DAYS LATER.

✎ **Look in the Bible story for the answers to these questions.**

1. Who tied up Jesus and took him to Pilate?

2. Who spit on Jesus and hit him?

3. What did Jesus say when they were so mean to him?

THE BIBLE TELLS ABOUT BEING SELF-DISCIPLINED

Jesus Is Quiet When People Make Fun of Him

✎ **Read about Jesus in your Bible in Matthew 27:1-31, John 19:16-42, or on pages 36 and 37. Put the words from the WORD BOX in the puzzle and then write them in the sentences about the Bible story.**

11 L E A D E R S

8 J E S U S

WORD BOX:

anything
crucified
Golgotha
soldiers
leaders
Jesus
crown
governor
trouble
Pilate
Joseph
garden

1. The _____ said Jesus should be _____ ;
   ₁₁   ₇

they said he was causing _____ with the people.
                            ₁

2. _____ was tied up and taken to _____ ,
   ₈   ₄

the _____ .
    ₆

3. The _____ made fun of Jesus and put a _____
       ₃   ₁₂

of thorns on his head, but he didn't say _____ .
                                            ₉

4. They took Jesus to _____ and he died there.
                        ₅

5. _____ put Jesus' body in a tomb in a _____ .
   ₁₀   ₂

SELF-DISCIPLINE WHEN SOMETHING GOES WRONG

What do you do when something goes wrong? That may be a good time to practice self-discipline. Being self-disciplined sometimes means being quiet. But it can also mean speaking up when you need to. ✎ **Read each situation, then write what each person could do to show they are growing in self-discipline.**

Laura studied for the test but she still didn't get a good grade.

_____
_____
_____
_____

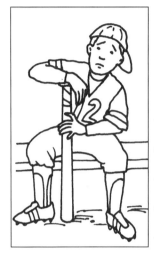

Zach's team lost the championship game.

_____
_____
_____
_____

Troy can't find the homework he did last night.

_____
_____
_____
_____

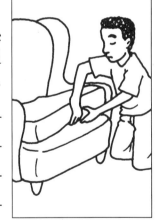

Janine's friend didn't do what she promised to do.

_____
_____
_____
_____

What are some things you should NOT do when things go wrong?

1. Hit someone.
2. Yell at the other person.
3. Blame someone if you did it.
4. _____

What are some things you CAN do when things go wrong?

1. Pray.
2. Talk to a trusted adult.
3. Start over.
4. _____

WORDS ABOUT SELF-DISCIPLINE

There are a lot of words to help us think about being self-disciplined. ✎ **Look for these words in the word search below and color in the letters for each one when you find it. Some letters may be in more than one word.**

best	better	courage	desire	endure	give
God	good	honor	improve	love	me
practice	pray	respect	strong	think	train
try	want	wisdom	work	self-disciplined	

```
Y  A  R  P  W  O  R  K  J  K  F  D  O  O  G  T
R  Z  K  G  I  Q  P  L  J  M  N  D  Q  G  B  H
E  M  N  H  S  D  F  W  A  N  T  F  E  M  V  I
S  E  L  F  D  I  S  C  I  P  L  I  N  E  D  N
P  Q  D  H  O  M  B  N  P  R  W  G  D  X  E  K
E  F  G  O  M  P  M  B  V  A  R  W  U  C  S  S
C  P  J  N  N  R  D  B  G  C  Q  W  R  K  I  H
T  R  Y  O  Q  O  B  E  S  T  N  P  E  T  R  A
W  Q  K  R  M  V  S  T  J  I  V  X  Z  R  E  R
F  J  G  I  V  E  X  T  Q  C  O  U  R  A  G  E
E  V  O  L  K  J  Q  E  M  E  C  N  X  I  J  G
P  Z  D  J  W  Q  C  R  V  S  T  R  O  N  G  M
```

✎ **Write the words from the word search that can help you be self-disciplined when . . .**

1. Your friend went somewhere you wanted to go and didn't ask you to go.

2. You don't want to get out of your warm bed to get ready for school.

3. You want to play volleyball, but no one else does.

TRIANGLE BEADS AND TOOTHPICK SCULPTURES

When you keep at a project that takes lots of time and careful work, you are learning to be self-disciplined. Try one of these projects and keep working until you are finished!

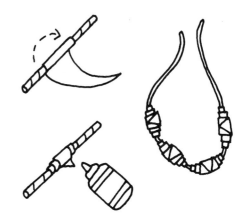

TRIANGLE BEADS

You need:
- ☐ 2-3 different colors of construction paper
- ☐ Scissors
- ☐ White glue
- ☐ Cardboard pattern, cut into a triangle 4-5" long and with 1-1/2" base
- ☐ 18" length of yarn or string
- ☐ Drinking straw or knitting needle
- ☐ OPTIONAL: Glitter, small beads, and paints

✂ To make Triangle Beads:
1. Use the cardboard pattern and cut out 12-15 triangles, using one or more colors as you wish.
2. Make a bead by starting at the base (1-1/2" side) of the triangle and rolling the paper tightly around the straw or knitting needle.
3. Put a few drops of glue over and under the tip of the triangle and hold it in place so it won't unroll. Leave it to dry for a few minutes while you make another bead.
4. After you have made all the beads and the glue is dry, string the beads on the yarn, tie the ends of the yarn together, and wear your beads!
5. OPTIONAL: Beads can be decorated with glitter or paint before you string them on the yarn.

TOOTHPICK SCULPTURE

I'M GOING TO HIDE IN THE TOOTHPICK SCULPTURE.

MAYBE THEY'LL PAINT YOU TO MATCH IT!

You need:
- ☐ 25 or more miniature marshmallows
- ☐ 50 or more toothpicks

✂ To make a Toothpick Sculpture:
1. Use the marshmallows to be the joints between the toothpicks.
2. Connect the toothpicks with marshmallows in between and expand your sculpture in as many directions as you can.
3. Be sure to design a base on the sculpture so it can stand up.

THE VALUE OF BEING SELF-DISCIPLINED

God's values are the STANDARD to help me know how to live my life and treat other people

HOW CAN YOU KNOW WHAT YOUR VALUES ARE? Look at the things you DO, SAY, and THINK. If you spend time doing something, then you know it is one of your values.

I want God's values to become my values.

Are you thinking what is in the thought balloon?

My name is _____.

Being self-disciplined _____ important to me.
is   is not

I _____ spend time doing what I know I should do, even when

I don't feel like it.
do   do not

Making myself do what I know I should do even when I don't feel like doing it is being self-disciplined.

I can show that being self-disciplined is becoming my value when I _____

_____ and _____

✎   **Use small cards to write four things you need to remember to do this week. Decorate a box and put the cards inside. During the week read the cards and practice being self-disciplined by doing what's on each.**

VALUE BUILDERS SERIES INDEX
BY VALUE

Accepting
Romans 15:7
Galatians 3:28
Luke 7 — Jesus and the woman with no name
Acts 10 — Peter's vision and visit

Appreciative
See thankful

Attentive
Psalm 34:15
James 1:19
Nehemiah 8 — Ezra reads the law
Luke 10 — Mary listens to Jesus

Caring
See concerned

Choices
See wise

Committed
1 Kings 8:61
Proverbs 16:3
Esther 4 — Esther
John 1 — Andrew follows Jesus

Compassionate
2 Corinthians 1:3-4
1 Peter 3:8
Luke 10 — Good Samaritan
Luke 23 — Jesus on the cross

Concerned
1 Corinthians 12:25
1 John 3:17
Matthew 25 — Jesus teaches to meet needs
Acts 2 — Church provides for each other

Confident
Philippians 4:13
Psalm 139:14
1 Samuel 17 — David and Goliath
Nehemiah 6 — Nehemiah isn't intimidated

Considerate
See respectful, kind

Consistent
1 John 3:18
Psalm 33:4
Matthew 26 — Jesus in the garden
Daniel 6 — Daniel as administrator

Contented
See peaceful

Conviction
Deuteronomy 13:6-8
Acts 4:19-20
Daniel 3 — Blazing furnace and three Hebrews
John 2 — Jesus clears the temple courts

Cooperative
Colossians 3:23-24
Ephesians 4:16
Acts 6 — Disciples share responsibilities
Exodus 18 — Jethro gives Moses a plan

Courageous
Joshua 1:9
Isaiah 41:10
Acts 23 — Paul's nephew
Esther 4 — Esther

Creative
See resourceful

Decision Making
See purposeful

Dedicated
See committed

Dependable
See responsible

Diligent
See persevering, purposeful, responsible

Discerning
See wise

Discipleship
See teachable, prayerful, worshipful, faith, holy

Discipline
See self-disciplined

Empathy
Galatians 6:2
Hebrews 13:3
John 11 — Jesus at Lazarus's death
1 Samuel 19 — Jonathan speaks up for David

Endurance
See persevering, self-disciplined, purposeful

Enthusiasm
See joyful

Fairness
Leviticus 19:15
Romans 12:17
James 2 — Favoritism at a meeting
Matthew 20 — Parable of workers

Faith
John 3:16
Hebrews 11:6
Acts 16 — Philippian jailer
Matthew 8 — Centurion sends servant to Jesus

Faithful
See loyal

VALUE BUILDERS SERIES INDEX
BY VALUE

Fellowship
See friendly

Flexibility
See cooperative, initiative, resourceful

Forgiving
Ephesians 4:32
Leviticus 19:18
Matthew 18 — Parable of unforgiving servant
Genesis 45 — Joseph forgives brothers

Friendly
Luke 6:31
Proverbs 17:17
1 Samuel 18 — David and Jonathan
Acts 9 — Paul and Barnabas

Generosity
Matthew 5:42
Hebrews 13:16
Ruth 2 — Boaz gives grain to Ruth
2 Corinthians 8 — Paul's letter about sharing

Gentle
Matthew 11:29-30
Philippians 4:5
Mark 10 — Jesus and the children
John 19 — Joseph of Arimathea prepares Jesus' body

Genuineness
See sincerity

Giving
See generosity

Goodness
See consistent, holy

Helpfulness
Acts 20:35
Ephesians 6:7-8
Exodus 2 — Miriam and baby Moses
Mark 14 — Disciples prepare Last Supper

Holy
1 Peter 1:15
Psalm 51:10
Acts 10 — Cornelius
Exodus 3 — Moses and the burning bush

Honest
Leviticus 19:11
Ephesians 4:25
Mark 14 — Peter lies about knowing Jesus
1 Samuel 3 — Samuel tells Eli the truth

Honor
See obedient, respectful, reverence

Hopeful
Jeremiah 29:11
Romans 15:13
Acts 1 — Jesus will return/Ascension
Genesis 15 — Abraham looks to the future

Humble
Psalm 25:9
Romans 12:16
Luke 7 — Centurion asks Jesus to heal son
Matthew 3 — John the Baptist and Jesus

Independent
See confident, initiative

Initiative
Joshua 22:5
Ephesians 4:29
John 13 — Jesus washes feet
Nehemiah 2 — Nehemiah asks to go to Jerusalem

Integrity
See consistent, holy, honest

Joyful
1 Thessalonians 5:16
1 Peter 1:8
Luke 2 — Jesus' birth
Acts 12 — Rhoda greets Peter

Justice
See fairness

Kind
1 Thessalonians 5:15
Luke 6:35
2 Samuel 9 — David and Mephibosheth
Acts 28 — Malta islanders and Paul

Knowledge
See teachable

Listening
See attentive

Long-suffering
See patience

Loving
John 13:34-35
1 Corinthians 13:4-7
Luke 15 — Prodigal son
John 11 — Mary, Martha, Lazarus and Jesus

Loyal
1 Chronicles 29:18
Romans 12:5
1 Samuel 20 — David and Jonathan
Ruth 1 — Ruth and Naomi

Meek
See gentle, humble

Sympathy
See compassionate, concerned

Teachable
Joshua 1:8
Psalm 32:8
Luke 2   Young Jesus in the temple
Acts 18   Apollos with Priscilla and Aquila

Thankful
Psalm 28:17
Colossians 3:17
1 Chronicles 29   Celebrating the temple
Romans 16   Paul thanks Phoebe, Priscilla and
                          Aquila

Tolerant
See accepting

Trusting
Proverbs 3:5-6
Psalm 9:10
Acts 27   Sailors with Paul in shipwreck
2 Kings 18   Hezekiah trusts God

Trustworthiness
See honest, responsible

Truthful
See honest

Unselfish
Romans 15:1-3
Philippians 2:4
Luke 23   God gives His Son
John 6   Boy gives lunch

Wise
Proverbs 8:10
James 3:13
1 Kings 3   Solomon asks for wisdom
Daniel 1   Daniel and king's meat

Worshipful
Psalm 86:12
Psalm 122:1
Nehemiah 8   Ezra and the people worship
Acts 16   Paul and Silas in jail

VALUE BUILDERS SERIES INDEX
BY SCRIPTURE

Genesis 15	Abraham looks to future	Hopeful
Genesis 26	Isaac opens new wells	Patience
Genesis 45	Joseph forgives brothers	Forgiving
Exodus 2	Miriam and baby Moses	Helpful
Exodus 3	Moses and the burning bush	Holy
Exodus 5	Moses doesn't give up	Persevering
Exodus 18	Jethro gives Moses a plan	Cooperative
Leviticus 19:11		Honest
Leviticus 19:15		Fairness
Leviticus 19:18		Forgiving
Numbers 13	Caleb follows instructions	Responsible
Deuteronomy 5:16		Respectful
Deuteronomy 13:6-8		Conviction
Joshua 1:8		Teachable
Joshua 1:9		Courageous
Joshua 22:5		Initiative
Joshua 24	Joshua serves God	Purposeful
Ruth 1	Ruth and Naomi	Loyal
Ruth 2	Boaz gives grain to Ruth	Generosity
1 Samuel 3	Samuel tells Eli the truth	Honest
1 Samuel 15:22		Obedient
1 Samuel 17	David and Goliath	Confident
1 Samuel 17	David takes lunch	Obedient
1 Samuel 18	David and Jonathan	Friendly
1 Samuel 19	Jonathan speaks up for David	Empathy
1 Samuel 20	David and Jonathan	Loyal
1 Samuel 25	Abigail helps David show mercy	Merciful
1 Samuel 26	David doesn't kill Saul	Respectful
2 Samuel 9	David and Mephibosheth	Kind
1 Kings 3	Solomon asks for wisdom	Wise
1 Kings 8:61		Committed
2 Kings 18	Hezekiah trusts God	Trusting
1 Chronicles 29	Celebrating the temple	Thankful
1 Chronicles 29:18		Loyal
2 Chronicles 31	Temple contributions	Stewardship
Nehemiah 2	Nehemiah asks to go to Jerusalem	Initiative
Nehemiah 6	Nehemiah isn't intimidated	Confident
Nehemiah 6	Nehemiah stands firm	Patience
Nehemiah 8	Ezra and the people worship	Worshipful
Nehemiah 8	Ezra reads the law	Attentive
Esther 4	Esther	Committed
Esther 4	Esther	Courageous
Job 33:3		Sincerity

Psalm 9:10		Trusting
Psalm 25:9		Humble
Psalm 28:17		Thankful
Psalm 32:8		Teachable
Psalm 33:4		Consistent
Psalm 34:15		Attentive
Psalm 37:7		Patience
Psalm 51:10		Holy
Psalm 78:4, 7		Reverence
Psalm 86:12		Worshipful
Psalm 103:10		Merciful
Psalm 122:1		Worshipful
Psalm 139:14		Confident
Proverbs 3:5-6		Trusting
Proverbs 8:10		Wise
Proverbs 16:3		Committed
Proverbs 17:17		Friendly
Proverbs 20:11		Responsible
Isaiah 41:10		Courageous
Jeremiah 29:11		Hopeful
Daniel 1	Daniel and king's meat	Self-disciplined
Daniel 1	Daniel and king's meat	Wise
Daniel 3	Blazing furnace and three Hebrews	Conviction
Daniel 3	Blazing furnace and three Hebrews	Reverence
Daniel 6	Daniel as administrator	Consistent
Daniel 6	Daniel prays daily	Prayerful
Daniel 6:26-27		Reverence
Micah 6:8		Merciful
Matthew 3	John the Baptist and Jesus	Humble
Matthew 5:42		Generosity
Matthew 6	Jesus teaches contentment	Peaceful
Matthew 8	Centurion sends servant to Jesus	Faith
Matthew 11:29-30		Gentle
Matthew 18	Unmerciful servant	Merciful
Matthew 18	Parable of unforgiving servant	Forgiving
Matthew 20	Parable of workers	Fairness
Matthew 21	Triumphal entry	Reverence
Matthew 25	Jesus teaches to meet needs	Concerned
Matthew 26	Jesus in Gethsemane	Purposeful
Matthew 26	Jesus in the garden	Consistent
Mark 5	Jairus and his daughter	Sincerity
Mark 10	Jesus and the children	Gentle
Mark 14	Disciples prepare Last Supper	Helpful
Mark 14	Peter lies about knowing Jesus	Honest
Luke 2	Jesus' birth	Joyful
Luke 2	Young Jesus in the temple	Teachable
Luke 3:11		Stewardship
Luke 5	Man lowered through roof	Resourceful
Luke 6:31		Friendly
Luke 6:35		Kind

Luke 7	Centurion asks Jesus to heal son	Humble	1 Corinthians 12:25		Concerned
Luke 7	Jesus and woman with no name	Accepting	1 Corinthians 13:4-7		Loving
Luke 10	Good Samaritan	Compassionate	1 Corinthians 15:58		Purposeful
Luke 10	Mary listens to Jesus	Attentive			
Luke 11	Jesus teaches disciples	Prayerful	2 Corinthians 1:3-4		Compassionate
Luke 15	Prodigal son	Loving	2 Corinthians 8	Paul's letter about sharing	Generosity
Luke 15	Prodigal son	Repentant			
Luke 19	Zacchaeus	Resourceful	Galatians 3:28		Accepting
Luke 22	Peter's denial	Repentant	Galatians 6:2		Empathy
Luke 23	God gives His Son	Unselfish	Galatians 6:4-5		Responsible
Luke 23	Jesus on the cross	Compassionate	Galatians 6:9		Persevering
John 1	Andrew follows Jesus	Committed	Ephesians 4:2		Patience
John 2	Jesus clears the temple courts	Conviction	Ephesians 4:16		Cooperative
John 3:16		Faith	Ephesians 4:25		Honest
John 6	Boy gives lunch	Unselfish	Ephesians 4:29		Initiative
John 11	Jesus at Lazarus's death	Empathy	Ephesians 4:32		Forgiving
John 11	Mary, Martha, Lazarus, and Jesus	Loving	Ephesians 5:15-16		Stewardship
John 13	Jesus washes feet	Initiative	Ephesians 6:1		Obedient
John 13:34-35		Loving	Ephesians 6:7-8		Helpful
John 14:27		Peaceful			
John 19	Jesus is mocked	Self-disciplined	Philippians 2:4		Unselfish
John 19	Joseph of Arimathea prepares Jesus' body	Gentle	Philippians 4:5		Gentle
			Philippians 4:6		Prayerful
			Philippians 4:9		Resourceful
Acts 1	Jesus will return/Ascension	Hopeful	Philippians 4:13		Confident
Acts 2	Church provides for each other	Concerned			
Acts 4	Believers share	Stewardship	Colossians 3:17		Thankful
Acts 4:19-20		Conviction	Colossians 3:23-24		Cooperative
Acts 6	Disciples share responsibilities	Cooperative			
Acts 9	Ananias at Saul's conversion	Obedient	1 Thessalonians 5:15		Kind
Acts 9	Paul and Barnabas	Friendly	1 Thessalonians 5:16		Joyful
Acts 10	Cornelius	Holy	1 Timothy 4:7-8		Self-disciplined
Acts 10	Peter's vision and visit	Accepting			
Acts 12	Peter sleeping in prison	Peaceful	2 Timothy 1	Timothy	Sincerity
Acts 12	Rhoda greets Peter	Joyful	2 Timothy 1:7		Self-disciplined
Acts 16	Paul and Silas in jail	Worshipful			
Acts 16	Philippian jailer	Faith	Hebrews 11:6		Faith
Acts 16	Lydia and other believers	Respectful	Hebrews 13:3		Empathy
Acts 18	Apollos with Priscilla and Aquila	Teachable	Hebrews 13:5-6		Peaceful
Acts 20	Paul continues his work	Responsible	Hebrews 13:16		Generosity
Acts 20:35		Helpful			
Acts 23	Paul's nephew	Courageous	James 1:2-3		Persevering
Acts 26:20		Repentant	James 1:19		Attentive
Acts 27	Paul in a shipwreck	Persevering	James 1:22		Purposeful
Acts 27	Sailors with Paul in shipwreck	Trusting	James 2	Favoritism at a meeting	Fairness
Acts 28	Malta islanders with Paul	Kind	James 3:13		Wise
			James 5:16		Prayerful
Romans 12:5		Loyal			
Romans 12:9		Sincerity	1 Peter 1:8		Joyful
Romans 12:16		Humble	1 Peter 1:15		Holy
Romans 12:17		Fairness	1 Peter 2:17		Respectful
Romans 15:1-3		Unselfish	1 Peter 3:8		Compassionate
Romans 15:7		Accepting	1 Peter 4:10		Resourceful
Romans 15:13		Hopeful			
Romans 16	Paul thanks Phoebe, Priscilla, and Aquila	Thankful	1 John 1:9		Repentant
			1 John 3:17		Concerned
			1 John 3:18		Consistent